STAR TREK

™

MAD LIBS®

by Eric Luper

PSS!
PRICE STERN SLOAN

An Imprint of Penguin Random House

PRICE STERN SLOAN
Penguin Young Readers Group
An Imprint of Penguin Random House LLC

Mad Libs format copyright © 2016 by Price Stern Sloan,
an imprint of Penguin Random House LLC. All rights reserved.

TM & © 2016 CBS Studios Inc. STAR TREK and related marks and logos
are trademarks of CBS Studios Inc. All Rights Reserved.

Concept created by Roger Price & Leonard Stern

Published by Price Stern Sloan,
an imprint of Penguin Random House LLC,
345 Hudson Street, New York, New York 10014.
Printed in the USA.

ISBN 978-0-8431-8364-1
1 3 5 7 9 10 8 6 4 2

MAD LIBS®

INSTRUCTIONS

MAD LIBS® is a game for people who don't like games! It can be played by one, two, three, four, or forty.

• RIDICULOUSLY SIMPLE DIRECTIONS

In this tablet you will find stories containing blank spaces where words are left out. One player, the READER, selects one of these stories. The READER does not tell anyone what the story is about. Instead, he/she asks the other players, the WRITERS, to give him/her words. These words are used to fill in the blank spaces in the story.

• TO PLAY

The READER asks each WRITER in turn to call out a word—an adjective or a noun or whatever the space calls for—and uses them to fill in the blank spaces in the story. The result is a MAD LIBS® game.

When the READER then reads the completed MAD LIBS® game to the other players, they will discover that they have written a story that is fantastic, screamingly funny, shocking, silly, crazy, or just plain dumb—depending upon which words each WRITER called out.

• EXAMPLE (*Before* and *After*)

"_____!" he said _____
　　　　EXCLAMATION　　　　　　　　　　　　　　ADVERB

as he jumped into his convertible _____ and
　　　　　　　　　　　　　　　　　　　　　　　NOUN

drove off with his _____ wife.
　　　　　　　　　ADJECTIVE

"_____**OUCH**_____!" he said _____**STUPIDLY**_____
　　　　EXCLAMATION　　　　　　　　　　　　　　ADVERB

as he jumped into his convertible _____**CAT**_____ and
　　　　　　　　　　　　　　　　　　　　　　　NOUN

drove off with his _____**BRAVE**_____ wife.
　　　　　　　　　ADJECTIVE

QUICK REVIEW

In case you have forgotten what adjectives, adverbs, nouns, and verbs are, here is a quick review:

An ADJECTIVE describes something or somebody. *Lumpy, soft, ugly, messy,* and *short* are adjectives.

An ADVERB tells how something is done. It modifies a verb and usually ends in "ly." *Modestly, stupidly, greedily,* and *carefully* are adverbs.

A NOUN is the name of a person, place, or thing. *Sidewalk, umbrella, bridle, bathtub,* and *nose* are nouns.

A VERB is an action word. *Run, pitch, jump,* and *swim* are verbs. Put the verbs in past tense if the directions say PAST TENSE. *Ran, pitched, jumped,* and *swam* are verbs in the past tense.

When we ask for A PLACE, we mean any sort of place: a country or city (*Spain, Cleveland*) or a room (*bathroom, kitchen*).

An EXCLAMATION or SILLY WORD is any sort of funny sound, gasp, grunt, or outcry, like *Wow!, Ouch!, Whomp!, Ick!,* and *Gadzooks!*

When we ask for specific words, like a NUMBER, a COLOR, an ANIMAL, or a PART OF THE BODY, we mean a word that is one of those things, like *seven, blue, horse,* or *head.*

When we ask for a PLURAL, it means more than one. For example, *cat* pluralized is *cats.*

MAD LIBS® is fun to play with friends, but you can also play it by yourself! To begin with, DO NOT look at the story on the page below. Fill in the blanks on this page with the words called for. Then, using the words you have selected, fill in the blank spaces in the story.

Now you've created your own hilarious MAD LIBS® game!

THE MOST FAMOUS INTRO EVER

A PLACE _____

NOUN _____

SILLY WORD _____

NUMBER _____

VERB _____

PLURAL NOUN _____

NOUN _____

PLURAL NOUN _____

ANIMAL _____

ADJECTIVE _____

MAD LIBS®
THE MOST FAMOUS INTRO EVER

_____, the final _____. These are the voyages
  A PLACE   NOUN

of the Starship _____. Its _____-year mission:
                   SILLY WORD   NUMBER

to _____ strange new _____, to seek out new
      VERB   PLURAL NOUN

_____ and new _____, to boldly go where no
  NOUN   PLURAL NOUN

_____ has gone before!
  ANIMAL

[Cue: _____ music.]
           ADJECTIVE

From STAR TREK MAD LIBS® • TM & © 2016 CBS Studios Inc. STAR TREK and related marks
and logos are trademarks of CBS Studios Inc. All Rights Reserved. Published by Price Stern Sloan,
an imprint of Penguin Random House LLC, 345 Hudson Street, New York, NY 10014.

MAD LIBS® is fun to play with friends, but you can also play it by yourself! To begin with, DO NOT look at the story on the page below. Fill in the blanks on this page with the words called for. Then, using the words you have selected, fill in the blank spaces in the story.

Now you've created your own hilarious MAD LIBS® game!

WELCOME TO STARFLEET ACADEMY

VERB _____

VERB ENDING IN "ING" _____

PLURAL NOUN _____

NUMBER _____

NOUN _____

ADJECTIVE _____

TYPE OF LIQUID _____

VERB _____

SAME VERB _____

NOUN _____

ARTICLE OF CLOTHING _____

COLOR _____

ADJECTIVE _____

ADJECTIVE _____

PLURAL NOUN _____

CELEBRITY _____

PLURAL NOUN _____

MAD LIBS®
WELCOME TO STARFLEET ACADEMY

Before you set your phasers to _____, you've got a lot to
_____VERB_____

do before _____ Starfleet Academy. First of all, you'll
VERB ENDING IN "ING"

have to leave your old _____ behind. If you're going to
PLURAL NOUN

spend _____ years in space, you need to start with a clean
NUMBER

_____. Second, get ready to work. It's not all exotic,
NOUN

_____ aliens and Romulan _____. You need to
ADJECTIVE   TYPE OF LIQUID

_____—and to _____ hard. Eventually, you will be
VERB   SAME VERB

divided into groups and given a/an _____. That determines
NOUN

the color _____ you'll have to wear. Pray you don't get
ARTICLE OF CLOTHING

a/an _____ one or you're as good as _____. But life
COLOR   ADJECTIVE

at Starfleet Academy is not _____ all the time. You'll meet all
ADJECTIVE

kinds of new _____. And remember, hotshots such as James
PLURAL NOUN

T. Kirk and _____ have passed through these _____.
CELEBRITY   PLURAL NOUN

You could be next. Welcome to Starfleet Academy!

From STAR TREK MAD LIBS® • TM & © 2016 CBS Studios Inc. STAR TREK and related marks
and logos are trademarks of CBS Studios Inc. All Rights Reserved. Published by Price Stern Sloan,
an imprint of Penguin Random House LLC, 345 Hudson Street, New York, NY 10014.

MAD LIBS® is fun to play with friends, but you can also play it by yourself! To begin with, DO NOT look at the story on the page below. Fill in the blanks on this page with the words called for. Then, using the words you have selected, fill in the blank spaces in the story.

Now you've created your own hilarious MAD LIBS® game!

THE *KOBAYASHI MARU*

ADJECTIVE _____

A PLACE _____

NOUN _____

VERB _____

ADJECTIVE _____

PLURAL NOUN _____

NOUN _____

ADJECTIVE _____

NOUN _____

ADJECTIVE _____

NOUN _____

PLURAL NOUN _____

PERSON IN ROOM _____

NOUN _____

ADJECTIVE _____

ADEJCTIVE _____

VERB _____

NOUN _____

The most _____ challenge you will encounter in your
                ADJECTIVE

training at Starfleet _____ is the *Kobayashi Maru*. This
                        A PLACE

_____ will test your ability to _____ under pressure
   NOUN   VERB

and make _____ decisions. All _____ who want
            ADJECTIVE   PLURAL NOUN

to be in command must take this dreaded _____. The
                                            NOUN

_____ vessel, *Kobayashi Maru*, is stranded in the Klingon
  ADJECTIVE

Neutral _____. Cadets must decide whether to leave the
            NOUN

_____ civilians to certain death or attempt a rescue, which
  ADJECTIVE

would endanger their own _____ and the lives of all crew
                            NOUN

members. Either way, everyone ends up blown to _____! The
                                                  PLURAL NOUN

only person to ever defeat the *Kobayashi Maru* was _____,
                                                      PERSON IN ROOM

who reprogrammed the _____ so that the test could be
                        NOUN

beaten. Many consider this solution to be _____, but that
                                            ADJECTIVE

cadet received a commendation for " _____ thinking." Most
                                      ADJECTIVE

cadets _____ the *Kobayashi Maru*. How would you do in this
          VERB

no-win _____?
          NOUN

MAD LIBS® is fun to play with friends, but you can also play it by yourself! To begin with, DO NOT look at the story on the page below. Fill in the blanks on this page with the words called for. Then, using the words you have selected, fill in the blank spaces in the story.

Now you've created your own hilarious MAD LIBS® game!

PACKING LIST FOR A FIVE-YEAR MISSION

NOUN _____

ADJECTIVE _____

ADJECTIVE _____

NOUN _____

ADJECTIVE _____

NOUN _____

ADVERB _____

NOUN _____

ADJECTIVE _____

PLURAL NOUN _____

VERB _____

PLURAL NOUN _____

A PLACE _____

MAD LIBS®
PACKING LIST FOR A
FIVE-YEAR MISSION

If you are planning to go on a five-year _____, you'll need
                                              NOUN
to be sure to bring along some _____ items. Here are a few
                                    ADJECTIVE
things not to forget:

- _____ underwear: It is very cold in space.
      ADJECTIVE

- Favorite snacks: The replicator food can have a funny _____.
                                                            NOUN

- Books: It's very _____ on the holodeck.
                        ADJECTIVE

- Extra money: Romulan _____ doesn't come _____!
                            NOUN   ADVERB

- A journal: You'll want to keep track of every _____ you see.
                                                      NOUN

- More snacks: Really, that replicator food is _____.
                                                    ADJECTIVE

- Clothing from all _____ and times: You never know when
                        PLURAL NOUN

  you'll have to _____ back in time.
                      VERB

Also, be sure to leave all red _____ at (the) _____.
                                   PLURAL NOUN   A PLACE

You don't want to be mistaken for a redshirt!

MAD LIBS® is fun to play with friends, but you can also play it by yourself! To begin with, DO NOT look at the story on the page below. Fill in the blanks on this page with the words called for. Then, using the words you have selected, fill in the blank spaces in the story.

Now you've created your own hilarious MAD LIBS® game!

FAMOUS KLINGON PROVERBS

NUMBER _____

VERB _____

ADJECTIVE _____

NOUN _____

PART OF THE BODY (PLURAL) _____

NOUN _____

ANIMAL _____

NOUN _____

PLURAL NOUN _____

PLURAL NOUN _____

VERB _____

VERB _____

ADJECTIVE _____

SAME ADJECTIVE _____

ADJECTIVE _____

VERB _____

PLURAL NOUN _____

PART OF THE BODY _____

MAD LIBS
FAMOUS KLINGON PROVERBS

The Klingons have a very complex language and have had

_____ centuries to _____ some interesting sayings.
NUMBER   VERB

Here are a few _____ ones:
                 ADJECTIVE

- Revenge is a/an _____ best served cold.
                   NOUN

- Four thousand _____ may be cut in one
                 PART OF THE BODY (PLURAL)

  _____ by a running _____.
  NOUN   ANIMAL

- A leader is judged not by the length of his _____ but by the
                                               NOUN

  _____ he makes.
  PLURAL NOUN

- Pity the warrior who slays all his _____.
                                     PLURAL NOUN

- _____, and you may eat dinner. _____, and you
  VERB   VERB

  may *be* dinner.

- A/An _____ knife is nothing without a/an _____ eye.
       ADJECTIVE   SAME ADJECTIVE

- If winning is not _____, why keep score?
                    ADJECTIVE

- If you cannot control yourself, you cannot _____ others.
                                             VERB

So, if you meet a Klingon, use one of these _____ and you
                                            PLURAL NOUN

may keep your _____.
              PART OF THE BODY

MAD LIBS® is fun to play with friends, but you can also play it by yourself! To begin with, DO NOT look at the story on the page below. Fill in the blanks on this page with the words called for. Then, using the words you have selected, fill in the blank spaces in the story.

Now you've created your own hilarious MAD LIBS® game!

WHY KIRK IS A BETTER CAPTAIN THAN PICARD

VERB ENDING IN "ING" _____

NOUN _____

NOUN _____

ADVERB _____

A PLACE _____

VERB _____

NOUN _____

A PLACE _____

ANIMAL (PLURAL) _____

PART OF THE BODY (PLURAL) _____

VERB (PAST TENSE) _____

PLURAL NOUN _____

VERB _____

ADVERB _____

PART OF THE BODY _____

MAD LIBS®
WHY KIRK IS A BETTER CAPTAIN THAN PICARD

For years, scholars have been _____ over who is a better
                              VERB ENDING IN "ING"

_____, James Tiberius Kirk or Jean-Luc Picard. Well, the
      NOUN

_____ is _____ clear.
      NOUN   ADVERB

• Kirk brought Spock back from (the) _____.
                                         A PLACE

• Kirk does not _____ the flute.
                     VERB

• When Kirk screams at Khan, it echoes across the entire

_____.
     NOUN

• Kirk enabled the repopulation of (the) _____ with humpback
                                             A PLACE

_____.
ANIMAL (PLURAL)

• No one can roll on his _____ better than Kirk.
                         PART OF THE BODY (PLURAL)

• Kirk has _____ three computers by outthinking them.
            VERB (PAST TENSE)

• Kirk once made a cannon that shot _____.
                                       PLURAL NOUN

And of course...

• When they want to _____ to the *U.S.S. Enterprise*, Kirk
                        VERB

_____ snaps open his communicator while Picard pokes at his
 ADVERB

_____!
PART OF THE BODY

MAD LIBS® is fun to play with friends, but you can also play it by yourself! To begin with, DO NOT look at the story on the page below. Fill in the blanks on this page with the words called for. Then, using the words you have selected, fill in the blank spaces in the story.

Now you've created your own hilarious MAD LIBS® game!

THE REDSHIRT: A CAUTIONARY TALE

ARTICLE OF CLOTHING _____

NOUN _____

NOUN _____

OCCUPATION (PLURAL) _____

ADJECTIVE _____

VERB _____

VERB _____

NOUN _____

VERB _____

NOUN _____

PART OF THE BODY (PLURAL) _____

VERB _____

NUMBER _____

MAD LIBS
THE REDSHIRT:
A CAUTIONARY TALE

Everyone knows that if you are wearing a red _____ on

ARTICLE OF CLOTHING

the *U.S.S. Enterprise* and are asked to join the landing _____,

NOUN

you should make sure to fill out your last will and _____. In

NOUN

fact, 73 percent of all deaths occur to those _____ who

OCCUPATION (PLURAL)

are wearing red shirts. If you go to Starfleet Academy and are placed

in the engineering or security fields, here are a few _____ tips

ADJECTIVE

to stay alive.

1. Hide: If no one sees you, no one can _____ you to join the

VERB

   landing party.

2. Stand in the back: Let the redshirt in front of you _____

VERB

   a/an _____ to the chest.

NOUN

3. Duck!: Have you ever seen a redshirt _____ behind a/an

VERB

   _____ or do a shoulder roll?

NOUN

4. Keep your _____ crossed: Just because 73 percent

PART OF THE BODY (PLURAL)

   of redshirts _____, doesn't mean you have to be one of

VERB

   them. Be part of the _____ percent club!

NUMBER

From STAR TREK MAD LIBS® • TM & © 2016 CBS Studios Inc. STAR TREK and related marks
and logos are trademarks of CBS Studios Inc. All Rights Reserved. Published by Price Stern Sloan,
an imprint of Penguin Random House LLC, 345 Hudson Street, New York, NY 10014.

MAD LIBS® is fun to play with friends, but you can also play it by yourself! To begin with, DO NOT look at the story on the page below. Fill in the blanks on this page with the words called for. Then, using the words you have selected, fill in the blank spaces in the story.

Now you've created your own hilarious MAD LIBS® game!

THE CARE AND FEEDING OF YOUR TRIBBLE

VERB ENDING IN "ING" _____

PART OF THE BODY _____

ADJECTIVE _____

ADJECTIVE _____

VERB _____

VERB _____

ADVERB _____

NOUN _____

PLURAL NOUN _____

ADVERB _____

ADJECTIVE _____

ADJECTIVE _____

NOUN _____

NUMBER _____

NOUN _____

ANIMAL _____

MAD LIBS®
THE CARE AND FEEDING
OF YOUR TRIBBLE

If you are thinking of _____ a tribble, here is the first
                        VERB ENDING IN "ING"

rule of _____: DON'T! Tribbles are trouble, plain and
        PART OF THE BODY

_____. Sure, they are soft, cuddly, and _____
ADJECTIVE   ADJECTIVE

bundles of fur. Sure, they _____ when you pet them. And they
                          VERB

_____ every time they see a Klingon. But tribbles reproduce
VERB

_____ fast, and they eat huge amounts of _____.
ADVERB   NOUN

Dr. McCoy even said that their only two _____ in life are
                                        PLURAL NOUN

to eat and to reproduce, and they perform both of these functions

exceptionally _____. In fact, tribbles are so _____
              ADVERB   ADJECTIVE

that Starfleet has declared them _____ and prohibits their
                                 ADJECTIVE

_____. You might leave your cabin with one tribble and
NOUN

return a few hours later to find _____ tribbles—so many that
                                 NUMBER

the _____ could be overrun with them! So, do everyone a
    NOUN

favor and get a/an _____ instead.
                   ANIMAL

From STAR TREK MAD LIBS® • TM & © 2016 CBS Studios Inc. STAR TREK and related marks
and logos are trademarks of CBS Studios Inc. All Rights Reserved. Published by Price Stern Sloan,
an imprint of Penguin Random House LLC, 345 Hudson Street, New York, NY 10014.

MAD LIBS® is fun to play with friends, but you can also play it by yourself! To begin with, DO NOT look at the story on the page below. Fill in the blanks on this page with the words called for. Then, using the words you have selected, fill in the blank spaces in the story.

Now you've created your own hilarious MAD LIBS® game!

UH-OH, ROMULANS!

ADJECTIVE _____

ADJECTIVE _____

PLURAL NOUN _____

FIRST NAME _____

PART OF THE BODY (PLURAL) _____

COLOR _____

ADJECTIVE _____

TYPE OF LIQUID _____

ADVERB _____

ADJECTIVE _____

ADJECTIVE _____

PERSON IN ROOM _____

VERB _____

VERB _____

VERB _____

PART OF THE BODY _____

NOUN _____

EXCLAMATION _____

MAD LIBS

UH-OH, ROMULANS!

If Vulcans are _____ and logical, Romulans are the opposite.
                    ADJECTIVE

Cunning and _____, Romulans, who come from the twin
                ADJECTIVE

_____ of Romulus and _____, are usually at war
PLURAL NOUN   FIRST NAME

with the Federation. Romulans have pointed _____
                                            PART OF THE BODY (PLURAL)

and _____ blood, like Vulcans. However, they are nowhere
      COLOR

near as _____. Although illegal, Romulan _____ is
        ADJECTIVE   TYPE OF LIQUID

secretly traded in the Federation. But it will _____ give you
                                                ADVERB

a/an _____ headache. Romulans wear uniforms with _____
      ADJECTIVE   ADJECTIVE

shoulders, and their hair looks like something _____
                                               PERSON IN ROOM

might wear. Like the CIA, the Tal Shiar will do everything it can to

_____ you; and if all else fails, they will _____ you
VERB   VERB

with a swift _____ to the _____. Some say that
             VERB   PART OF THE BODY

Romulans and Vulcans share the same _____, but Mr. Spock
                                     NOUN

would say, " _____!"
             EXCLAMATION

MAD LIBS® is fun to play with friends, but you can also play it by yourself! To begin with, DO NOT look at the story on the page below. Fill in the blanks on this page with the words called for. Then, using the words you have selected, fill in the blank spaces in the story.

Now you've created your own hilarious MAD LIBS® game!

SO YOU WANT TO SLINGSHOT AROUND THE SUN?

SILLY WORD _____

ADJECTIVE _____

ADJECTIVE _____

A PLACE _____

ADVERB _____

PART OF THE BODY _____

ADJECTIVE _____

VERB ENDING IN "ING" _____

PLURAL NOUN _____

NOUN _____

PLURAL NOUN _____

VERB _____

ADJECTIVE _____

ADJECTIVE _____

ARTICLE OF CLOTHING _____

NOUN _____

MAD LIBS®
SO YOU WANT TO SLINGSHOT AROUND THE SUN?

Captains of the *U.S.S.* _____ sometimes have to travel
                  SILLY WORD

through time, but time travel is a/an _____ thing. First of all,
                             ADJECTIVE

if you go too fast or too _____, you could end up in the wrong
                  ADJECTIVE

_____. Plus, you need to make sure to blend in _____.
  A PLACE   ADVERB

A purple _____ would look _____ in 1930s New
         PART OF THE BODY   ADJECTIVE

York City! The Temporal Prime Directive prohibits the Federation

from _____ in historical _____. Once you
   VERB ENDING IN "ING"   PLURAL NOUN

change one _____, lots of other _____ can get
             NOUN   PLURAL NOUN

messed up. But the day may come when you have to _____
                                         VERB

back in time, and it's totally _____ that you are ready. So, put
                       ADJECTIVE

on your _____ old-time _____, and slingshot
        ADJECTIVE   ARTICLE OF CLOTHING

around the _____!
        NOUN

MAD LIBS® is fun to play with friends, but you can also play it by yourself! To begin with, DO NOT look at the story on the page below. Fill in the blanks on this page with the words called for. Then, using the words you have selected, fill in the blank spaces in the story.

Now you've created your own hilarious MAD LIBS® game!

A GUIDE TO VULCANS

ADJECTIVE _____

VERB _____

ADJECTIVE _____

PART OF THE BODY (PLURAL) _____

PART OF THE BODY _____

PLURAL NOUN _____

TYPE OF LIQUID _____

ADJECTIVE _____

ADJECTIVE _____

VERB _____

ADJECTIVE _____

ADJECTIVE _____

NOUN _____

NOUN _____

VERB _____

NOUN _____

PART OF THE BODY _____

MAD LIBS

A GUIDE TO VULCANS

Humans have a great deal of contact with Vulcans, so it is

_____ that you _____ as much as you can about
   ADJECTIVE   VERB

them. Everyone knows that Vulcans have _____ ears and
                                    ADJECTIVE

upswept _____. However, did you know a Vulcan's
       PART OF THE BODY (PLURAL)

heart is located between the ribs and _____? Vulcans
                             PART OF THE BODY

don't eat _____. They also don't drink _____, which
      PLURAL NOUN   TYPE OF LIQUID

is good because it makes them a little _____. Every seven
                          ADJECTIVE

years, Vulcans go through *Pon farr*, which is a/an _____ desire
                                 ADJECTIVE

to _____. No matter how _____ Vulcans are, there
   VERB   ADJECTIVE

is no avoiding it! Vulcans are about three times as _____ as
                                 ADJECTIVE

a human due to their planet's higher _____. They also don't
                        NOUN

need as much _____ as we do, since they evolved on a desert
          NOUN

planet. So, next time you _____ a Vulcan, give him or her
               VERB

a/an _____. Just don't let them pinch your _____!
   NOUN   PART OF THE BODY

MAD LIBS® is fun to play with friends, but you can also play it by yourself! To begin with, DO NOT look at the story on the page below. Fill in the blanks on this page with the words called for. Then, using the words you have selected, fill in the blank spaces in the story.

Now you've created your own hilarious MAD LIBS® game!

WELCOME TO THE BORG

ADJECTIVE _____

ADJECTIVE _____

VERB _____

ADJECTIVE _____

NOUN _____

ADVERB _____

VERB _____

PART OF THE BODY _____

VERB _____

NOUN _____

ADJECTIVE _____

ANIMAL (PLURAL) _____

PLURAL NOUN _____

ADVERB _____

NOUN _____

PLURAL NOUN _____

ADJECTIVE _____

From the moment you heard, "Resistance is _____," it was
ADJECTIVE

only a matter of time before your biological and _____
ADJECTIVE

distinctiveness would be added to our own. Now that you are part of

the Borg, you need to _____ a few things:
VERB

- The Unicomplex is the _____ base for the Borg. It is where
  ADJECTIVE

  the Borg _____ lives and where Borg cubes _____
  NOUN   ADVERB
  come and _____.
  VERB

- Your left _____ has been replaced with a sensor that
  PART OF THE BODY

  can _____ better than a human's. It also emits a red
  VERB

  _____, which looks pretty _____.
  NOUN   ADJECTIVE

- Borg are stronger than _____ and are immune to
  ANIMAL (PLURAL)

  _____, but we are not _____ good at running.
  PLURAL NOUN   ADVERB

- Forget thinking or any sort of _____. The Borg will do
  NOUN

  that for you. All you need to do is follow your _____.
  PLURAL NOUN

Welcome to the Borg. We hope your stay is a/an _____ one!
ADJECTIVE

MAD LIBS® is fun to play with friends, but you can also play it by yourself! To begin with, DO NOT look at the story on the page below. Fill in the blanks on this page with the words called for. Then, using the words you have selected, fill in the blank spaces in the story.

Now you've created your own hilarious MAD LIBS® game!

THE *ENTERPRISE*: A MAINTENANCE MANUAL

ADJECTIVE _____

ADJECTIVE _____

PLURAL NOUN _____

NOUN _____

VEHICLE _____

A PLACE _____

NOUN _____

PLURAL NOUN _____

SILLY WORD _____

NOUN _____

ADVERB _____

ADJECTIVE _____

NOUN _____

NUMBER _____

PLURAL NOUN _____

ADJECTIVE _____

NOUN _____

NUMBER _____

MAD LIBS
THE *ENTERPRISE*: A
MAINTENANCE MANUAL

Although Scotty makes taking care of the *Enterprise* look _____,
                                                            ADJECTIVE

it's actually quite a/an _____ job. First of all, you have to
                              ADJECTIVE

make sure you have enough dilithium _____ to run the warp
                                          PLURAL NOUN

_____. A/An _____ without warp capability is dead
    NOUN   VEHICLE

in (the) _____. You also need a dedicated _____ and
          A PLACE   NOUN

engineers who will stay at their _____ and do what they're
                                    PLURAL NOUN

told. The crew needs to keep the deck spick-and-_____.
                                                    SILLY WORD

The ship's _____ is made of duranium and tritanium, but
              NOUN

you _____ need some _____ aluminum for the
       ADVERB   ADJECTIVE

windows. Inspect the _____ often to make sure there's no
                         NOUN

damage. A starship costs _____ _____, so you have
                            NUMBER   PLURAL NOUN

to be _____. But with proper care and _____ of your
         ADJECTIVE   NOUN

starship, it will last you _____ years.
                              NUMBER

MAD LIBS® is fun to play with friends, but you can also play it by yourself! To begin with, DO NOT look at the story on the page below. Fill in the blanks on this page with the words called for. Then, using the words you have selected, fill in the blank spaces in the story.

Now you've created your own hilarious MAD LIBS® game!

HOW TO DEFEAT A GORN

ADJECTIVE _____

NUMBER _____

ADJECTIVE _____

VERB _____

ANIMAL _____

NOUN _____

ADJECTIVE _____

NOUN _____

SAME NOUN _____

CELEBRITY (MALE) _____

NOUN _____

PLURAL NOUN _____

VERB _____

ADVERB _____

ADJECTIVE _____

MAD LIBS

HOW TO DEFEAT A GORN

The Gorn are more _____ than humans in almost every
_____ADJECTIVE_____

way. They are _____ times stronger than humans and have
_____NUMBER_____

_____ skin. They are slower than us, which you can use to your
ADJECTIVE

advantage, but they don't _____ at all. Just because they look
_____VERB_____

like a/an _____, never underestimate their _____. In
_____ANIMAL_____   NOUN

fact, their _____ technology is almost as good as ours. Don't
_____ADJECTIVE_____

think of dropping a/an _____ on their heads, because it won't
_____NOUN_____

work—even a big _____! When Captain _____
_____SAME NOUN_____   CELEBRITY (MALE)

fought the Gorn, he managed to use a/an _____ stuffed with
_____NOUN_____

_____ and diamonds to stun the Gorn captain. Not even that
PLURAL NOUN

could _____ it for long! So, tread _____ around the
_____VERB_____   ADVERB

Gorn. They are tough and totally _____!
_____ADJECTIVE_____

MAD LIBS® is fun to play with friends, but you can also play it by yourself! To begin with, DO NOT look at the story on the page below. Fill in the blanks on this page with the words called for. Then, using the words you have selected, fill in the blank spaces in the story.

Now you've created your own hilarious MAD LIBS® game!

KHAAAAN!

PERSON IN ROOM _____

ADJECTIVE _____

NOUN _____

ADJECTIVE _____

NOUN _____

ADJECTIVE _____

VERB ENDING IN "ING" _____

NOUN _____

VERB _____

ADJECTIVE _____

ADVERB _____

VERB _____

ANIMAL _____

PLURAL NOUN _____

NOUN _____

VERB _____

MAD LIBS®

KHAAAAN!

Captain _____ once said that Khan was one of his most
_____PERSON IN ROOM_____

_____ adversaries. You wouldn't think so, considering
___ADJECTIVE___

the captain is from the twenty-third _____, but Khan is
_____NOUN_____

the product of _____ experiments and has a very high
_____ADJECTIVE_____

_____. He is also _____; Khan wouldn't think twice
___NOUN___   ___ADJECTIVE___

about _____ your whole family. If you awaken Khan from
___VERB ENDING IN "ING"___

suspended _____, he will _____ your entire crew.
_____NOUN_____   _____VERB_____

Even stranding him on a/an _____ planet won't stop him.
_____ADJECTIVE_____

Khan will find a way to _____ escape and _____
_____ADVERB_____   _____VERB_____

you. If you're not careful, he will even put a/an _____ in your
_____ANIMAL_____

ear and control your _____! So, if you are cruising around
_____PLURAL NOUN_____

Ceti Alpha V and are considering a trip to the planet's _____,
_____NOUN_____

_____ again!
_____VERB_____

MAD LIBS® is fun to play with friends, but you can also play it by yourself! To begin with, DO NOT look at the story on the page below. Fill in the blanks on this page with the words called for. Then, using the words you have selected, fill in the blank spaces in the story.

Now you've created your own hilarious MAD LIBS® game!

WHY PICARD IS BETTER THAN KIRK

PLURAL NOUN _____

NOUN _____

VERB _____

TYPE OF FOOD _____

ADJECTIVE _____

NOUN _____

ADVERB _____

ADJECTIVE _____

ADVERB _____

ANIMAL _____

VERB _____

COLOR _____

NOUN _____

NOUN _____

ADJECTIVE _____

PART OF THE BODY (PLURAL) _____

ADJECTIVE _____

PLURAL NOUN _____

MAD LIBS
WHY PICARD IS
BETTER THAN KIRK

Sure, you've heard all the _____ about why Kirk is better than
PLURAL NOUN

Picard, but what about the other side of the _____?
NOUN

• First, Picard can _____ more languages than Kirk and is an
VERB

 expert on fancy _____.
TYPE OF FOOD

• His ship is far more _____ than Kirk's ship.
ADJECTIVE

• Picard can fight with a/an _____ *and* he can _____
NOUN   ADVERB

 play the flute—maybe at the same time!

• Picard became part of the Borg. He had a/an _____ eye-
ADJECTIVE

 piece and everything, but still he _____ came back.
ADVERB

• Picard has never had a/an _____ problem on board, but
ANIMAL

 Kirk can't seem to _____ them.
VERB

• Not as many _____-shirts die under Picard's _____.
COLOR   NOUN

• Picard was never outsmarted by a/an _____ using a puppet.
NOUN

• No _____ sideburns... actually, no _____ at all!
ADJECTIVE   PART OF THE BODY (PLURAL)

So, don't be so _____ to pick Kirk as your favorite captain.
ADJECTIVE

Picard has some major-league _____ himself!
PLURAL NOUN

MAD LIBS® is fun to play with friends, but you can also play it by yourself! To begin with, DO NOT look at the story on the page below. Fill in the blanks on this page with the words called for. Then, using the words you have selected, fill in the blank spaces in the story.

Now you've created your own hilarious MAD LIBS® game!

YOUR STARFLEET MEDICAL TRAINING

ADJECTIVE _____

PLURAL NOUN _____

ADVERB _____

NOUN _____

ANIMAL _____

VERB _____

PLURAL NOUN _____

FIRST NAME (MALE) _____

OCCUPATION _____

COLOR _____

SAME COLOR _____

ARTICLE OF CLOTHING _____

ADJECTIVE _____

ADJECTIVE _____

PLURAL NOUN _____

MAD LIBS®
YOUR STARFLEET
MEDICAL TRAINING

Being a doctor for Starfleet is not as _____ as it looks. Not
                                       ADJECTIVE

only do you have to be an expert on human _____, you
                                           PLURAL NOUN

also have to be _____ familiar with many other forms of
                    ADVERB

_____. Federation doctors study human, Vulcan, Klingon,
    NOUN

and even _____ anatomy. They also have to be able to
            ANIMAL

_____ a medical tricorder all over the place and learn how
    VERB

to read all those wiggly _____. Another part of training is
                           PLURAL NOUN

learning to say, "He's dead, _____," and, "I'm a doctor,
                              FIRST NAME (MALE)

not a/an _____!" But if you have _____ eyes, you'll
            OCCUPATION   COLOR

be happy to know that you'll be able to wear a/an _____
                                                    SAME COLOR

_____ to match. The good news is that you'll be a/an
ARTICLE OF CLOTHING

_____ member of the crew and have a lot of _____
    ADJECTIVE   ADJECTIVE

contact with important _____. Welcome to Starfleet Medical.
                         PLURAL NOUN

Now, head down to sickbay!

MAD LIBS® is fun to play with friends, but you can also play it by yourself! To begin with, DO NOT look at the story on the page below. Fill in the blanks on this page with the words called for. Then, using the words you have selected, fill in the blank spaces in the story.

Now you've created your own hilarious MAD LIBS® game!

BEAM ME UP, SCOTTY!

ADJECTIVE _____

VERB ENDING IN "ING" _____

ADJECTIVE _____

NOUN _____

PART OF THE BODY _____

PLURAL NOUN _____

NUMBER _____

PLURAL NOUN _____

ADJECTIVE _____

ADJECTIVE _____

ADJECTIVE _____

VERB _____

NOUN _____

ADJECTIVE _____

ADVERB _____

MAD LIBS

BEAM ME UP, SCOTTY!

A cadet's first time in a transporter is a/an _____ experience.
ADJECTIVE

The thought of taking your body and _____ it into
VERB ENDING IN "ING"

_____ pieces just to reassemble it on the surface of a/an
ADJECTIVE

_____ boggles the _____! It only takes four or
NOUN   PART OF THE BODY

five _____ to transport somewhere. The trouble is that you
PLURAL NOUN

can only go _____ kilometers—less if you are transporting
NUMBER

through _____ or _____ layers of rock. Occasionally,
PLURAL NOUN   ADJECTIVE

there are _____ accidents. This occurs when the transporter
ADJECTIVE

fails and the subject experiences _____ injury or death. If
ADJECTIVE

you are a victim of a transporter accident, don't _____. The
VERB

transporter always keeps a/an _____ of the person for just
NOUN

such an occasion. If you're still _____, have no fear. You can
ADJECTIVE

always take the _____ slow route and fly a shuttlecraft. They
ADVERB

don't crash too often!

From STAR TREK MAD LIBS® • TM & © 2016 CBS Studios Inc. STAR TREK and related marks and logos are trademarks of CBS Studios Inc. All Rights Reserved. Published by Price Stern Sloan, an imprint of Penguin Random House LLC, 345 Hudson Street, New York, NY 10014.

MAD LIBS® is fun to play with friends, but you can also play it by yourself! To begin with, DO NOT look at the story on the page below. Fill in the blanks on this page with the words called for. Then, using the words you have selected, fill in the blank spaces in the story.

Now you've created your own hilarious MAD LIBS® game!

SEVEN OF NINE: THE PERILS OF BEING UNASSIMILATED

NOUN _____

NOUN _____

ADJECTIVE _____

VERB _____

ADVERB _____

PLURAL NOUN _____

ADJECTIVE _____

PLURAL NOUN _____

ADJECTIVE _____

VERB ENDING IN "ING" _____

PART OF THE BODY (PLURAL) _____

NOUN _____

ADJECTIVE _____

ADJECTIVE _____

TYPE OF FOOD _____

CELEBRITY _____

If you used to be part of the Borg _____ and have left the
                                      NOUN

collective, get ready for a shock to your _____. Both the
                                            NOUN

positive and _____ sides of humans may surprise you.
                 ADJECTIVE

Sometimes they _____ one way and then they do just the
                    VERB

opposite. It can be _____ confusing! Even though you may
                        ADVERB

be hundreds of _____ old, humans will still treat you like
                  PLURAL NOUN

a/an _____ child. Just because you don't understand their
        ADJECTIVE

_____, doesn't mean you're _____! You'll also have
  PLURAL NOUN   ADJECTIVE

to put up with people _____ at your ocular implant and
                        VERB ENDING IN "ING"

your bony _____. The rest of your _____
            PART OF THE BODY (PLURAL)   NOUN

could be _____, but they'll still stare. It's certain that you
            ADJECTIVE

will miss the collective, but over time you'll get more and more

_____. Walking among humans can be a challenge, but, hey,
  ADJECTIVE

they do have _____ and _____!
                TYPE OF FOOD   CELEBRITY

From STAR TREK MAD LIBS® • TM & © 2016 CBS Studios Inc. STAR TREK and related marks
and logos are trademarks of CBS Studios Inc. All Rights Reserved. Published by Price Stern Sloan,
an imprint of Penguin Random House LLC, 345 Hudson Street, New York, NY 10014.

MAD LIBS® is fun to play with friends, but you can also play it by yourself! To begin with, DO NOT look at the story on the page below. Fill in the blanks on this page with the words called for. Then, using the words you have selected, fill in the blank spaces in the story.

Now you've created your own hilarious MAD LIBS® game!

HOLODECK DOS AND DON'TS

PLURAL NOUN _____

VERB _____

NOUN _____

NOUN _____

ADJECTIVE _____

NOUN _____

TYPE OF FOOD _____

NOUN _____

VERB ENDING IN "ING" _____

ADVERB _____

VERB _____

VERB ENDING IN "ING" _____

ADJECTIVE _____

A PLACE _____

CELEBRITY _____

ADJECTIVE _____

MAD LIBS®
HOLODECK DOS AND DON'TS

There are certain _____ that you'll have to follow if you want
PLURAL NOUN

to _____ the holodeck. First of all, what is it? The holodeck is
VERB

a/an _____ that creates a simulated reality for anyone inside.
NOUN

The _____ the holodeck creates seems so _____
NOUN   ADJECTIVE

that you can hardly tell the difference! Eat a/an _____ in the
NOUN

holodeck and it tastes like _____! Want to play a game of
TYPE OF FOOD

_____? Strap on your helmet and start _____!
NOUN   VERB ENDING IN "ING"

People on starships _____ want to use the holodeck because
ADVERB

they can _____ things that they have not seen in months
VERB

or years. Some people like it so much that they can't stop themselves

from _____ it. That's called holodiction, and it's very
VERB ENDING IN "ING"

_____. So, if you're missing (the) _____ or want to
ADJECTIVE   A PLACE

meet _____, hop into the holodeck and get ready for some
CELEBRITY

_____ fun!
ADJECTIVE

MAD LIBS® is fun to play with friends, but you can also play it by yourself! To begin with, DO NOT look at the story on the page below. Fill in the blanks on this page with the words called for. Then, using the words you have selected, fill in the blank spaces in the story.

Now you've created your own hilarious MAD LIBS® game!

A TOUR OF DEEP SPACE 9

PERSON IN ROOM _____

NOUN _____

ADJECTIVE _____

NOUN _____

ADJECTIVE _____

NOUN _____

PLURAL NOUN _____

VERB _____

PLURAL NOUN _____

VERB _____

NOUN _____

ADJECTIVE _____

ANIMAL _____

VERB ENDING IN "ING" _____

ADJECTIVE _____

ARTICLE OF CLOTHING _____

ADJECTIVE _____

MAD LIBS
A TOUR OF DEEP SPACE 9

Being so close to the _____ wormhole and having access

<u>PERSON IN ROOM</u>

to the Gamma _____ brings a lot of _____ beings

<u>NOUN</u>   <u>ADJECTIVE</u>

to Deep Space 9, which is very exciting. It also allows for interstellar

_____ and _____ conflict! But life on a space

<u>NOUN</u>   <u>ADJECTIVE</u>

_____ isn't all excitement and _____. Starships come

<u>NOUN</u>   <u>PLURAL NOUN</u>

and _____, and you need to help nearby _____ on

<u>VERB</u>   <u>PLURAL NOUN</u>

a day-to-day basis. Plus, you have to _____ with the Ferengi

<u>VERB</u>

while dealing with the Founders who can change _____ at

<u>NOUN</u>

will. One day your buddy will be a/an _____ woman and the

<u>ADJECTIVE</u>

next day—a/an _____. But _____ with Captain

<u>ANIMAL</u>   <u>VERB ENDING IN "ING"</u>

Sisko and Commander Nerys all the time is totally _____. So,

<u>ADJECTIVE</u>

hang on to your _____ and get ready for the time of your

<u>ARTICLE OF CLOTHING</u>

life—_____ years on Deep Space 9!

<u>ADJECTIVE</u>

From STAR TREK MAD LIBS® • TM & © 2016 CBS Studios Inc. STAR TREK and related marks
and logos are trademarks of CBS Studios Inc. All Rights Reserved. Published by Price Stern Sloan,
an imprint of Penguin Random House LLC, 345 Hudson Street, New York, NY 10014.

Download Mad Libs today!

Join the millions of Mad Libs fans creating
wacky and wonderful stories on our apps!